Defend Your Profits

Safety Tools for Bottom Line Improvement

By Rodney Grieve

Published By:

BRANTA Worldwide
Sacramento, California
USA

ISBN 1-59196-162-9

BRANTA Worldwide
2443 Fair Oaks Blvd. #329
Sacramento, CA 95825
Phone 916.487.1919 • Toll Free 866.427.2682
Fax 916.487.1991

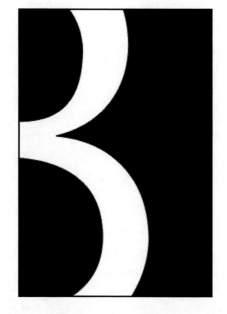

LEARN

BRANTA Worldwide

brant \ 'brant \ *n, pl* **brant** or **brants** [origin unknown]: a wild goose; *esp* : any of several small dark geese (genus **Branta**) that breed in the Arctic and migrate southward.

"When geese are on the ground, they wander around individually, ignore one another, scavenge for food, and look out for only themselves. When they are on the ground, they are known as a gaggle. When a gaggle takes flight, however, something magical happens: they fly in a formation known as a skein, and they fly 72% further and significantly faster than they do on their own. The honking that you hear is thought by scientists to be positive reinforcement for the leader to keep up the pace. When the lead goose gets tired, it falls back and another takes its place. When one of the geese is sick or injured, two birds accompany it to the ground until it recovers. Once it recovers, they accompany it back to the flock."

Do you want your organization to operate like a gaggle or a skein?

LEAD

About the Author

Rodney Grieve

Rodney Grieve is the founder of BRANTA Worldwide Inc, a firm dedicated to helping clients safely build quality products. He has nearly two decades of hands-on environmental compliance and health and safety experience, many of which he spent in the highly regulated hazardous waste industry. After years observing the flaws of traditional safety programs, Rodney developed The BRANTA Method™, a system designed to change the company culture. Implementation of the BRANTA Method™ has contributed to significant reductions in total incidents and actual injuries for many clients. The BRANTA Method™ focuses on the development of leadership skills in front-line supervisors so that they can work to actively defend their company profits and protect employees.

Mr. Grieve has authored three books in the Defend Your Profits series. He regularly speaks to managers at all levels about the significance of their role in creating a successful business culture. He holds a Master Degree in Environmental Policy and Management from the University of Denver and a Bachelor Degree in Biological Sciences from Cal Poly SLO. He is a Professional Member of the National Speakers Association and a Certified Instructor for the Dale Carnegie Organization. When Rodney isn't on the road, he enjoys spending time at his Northern California home with his wife, Darcy, and their two children, Hudson and McKinley.

SOAR

Table of Contents

If you committed unlimited funds to your safety program, would that guarantee zero injuries?

Defend Your Profits   8

Introduction

Your business is losing money to safety failures. In 1998, Liberty Mutual Insurance estimated that U.S. businesses pay $155 to $232 billion each year in direct and indirect costs for occupational injuries and illnesses.[1] Based on inflation, those numbers are now to $192 to $288 billion in 2006. Fortunately, you can minimize your safety losses. The tools identified in this guide will help you keep your hard-earned profits. Safety takes effort and commitment—it does not need to take all your money.

Although most safety professionals, consulting firms, and the U.S. Occupational Safety and Health Administration (Fed-OSHA) recommend extensive compliance audit programs and

---

[1] Liberty Mutual Workplace Safety Index, 1998.

expensive safety incentive plans, they are not the focus of this guide. Compliance with regulatory requirements protects you from fines and jail. It does not protect your employees from injury, and your profits from disappearing. Compliance with OSHA standards, although necessary, is the start of an effective safety process, not the end. And a safety incentive program, if not managed properly, can cost a small fortune and even *contribute* to your safety problems, leading to even more costs. After all, if **you committed unlimited funds to your safety program, would that guarantee zero injuries?**

Traditional safety management falls into one of three categories: compliance-based safety, behavior-based safety, and engineering-based safety. Each of these methods has value and elements of each are necessary for a successful process. However, each of these methods also has flaws. (See the Comparison Charts on pages 11 and 12) Of these flaws, the most critical is that each allows front-line supervisors to abdicate their responsibility to another entity or process. The BRANTA Method™ described in this book is a logic-based approach that promotes supervisor accountability for creating an environment of success…and gives them the tools to do so.

Type of Program	Focus	Main Goal	Driven by	Relationships
Compliance-Based Safety	On rules and regulatory programs only	Establish OSHA compliance	Safety professionals	Usually adversarial (i.e. safety cop) and confrontational
Behavior-Based Safety	On safe behaviors only	Correct unsafe behaviors	Employee committees	Although 'anonymous/no blame' system, focus is on employee actions
Engineering-Based Safety	On work processes only	Eliminate work place hazards	Safety engineers	Since work process based, does not involve personal relationships
Logic-Based Safety	On effective leadership and communication skills at the front-line supervisor level	Continually improve safety, productivity, and quality	Front-line supervisors	Builds positive working relationships to create overall business success by reducing turnover and improving morale

Type of Program	Supervisor's Role	Difficulty to Implement	Overall
Compliance-Based Safety	Lets supervisor abdicate responsibility to safety management team	Some initial training, but difficult to get compliance	Makes safety a negative and a necessary evil outside of definition of business success
Behavior-Based Safety	Lets supervisor abdicate responsibility to employees	Significant initial employee training and ongoing time and paperwork burden on employees	Misses process improvements and hazard elimination
Engineering-Based Safety	Lets supervisor abdicate responsibility to the work process	Significant business interruptions and large capital expenditures for work process modifications	Ignores the human element of business and the reality of cash flow
Logic-Based Safety	Creates supervisor accountability for creating an environment of success	Significant initial supervisor training and on-the-job practice	Integrates safety with productivity and quality to create a balanced culture of success

Safety success comes from accountability and responsibility throughout an organization, with front-line supervisors[2] in the lead. The next six chapters provide those supervisors the specific tools necessary to manage safety. The information contained in this book is not only for front-line supervisors, however. Whatever level you manage within your organization, implementing these simple tools will increase your profitability.

This book will not provide a "silver bullet" to stop safety failures; instead, it will help you gather and understand the information you need to manage your bottom line.

This book explains six realities of safety management. Each chapter contains *Get the Facts* questions that give you the opportunity to learn about and record pertinent data for your organization. Without this data, you cannot make sound business decisions. The *Quick Checks* worksheets help you quickly evaluate your company's overall safety performance so you can choose the direction you need to lead. Finally, a *Key Point* segment in each chapter highlights important information to help you soar as a leader.

---

[2] Throughout this guide, the term *supervisor* means any individual in an organization with front-line direct reports. These individuals may have job titles of manager, superintendent, leadman, or foreman. Regardless of the title, you can apply the principles discussed in this guide to any supervisor in any industry.

ICON KEY

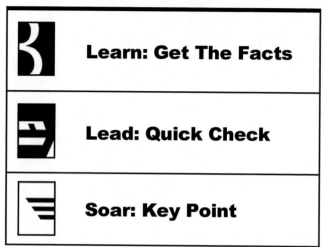

	Learn: Get The Facts
	Lead: Quick Check
	Soar: Key Point

With these tools you will identify and address your organization's safety issues. You will learn how to minimize your safety losses and **defend your profits.**

NOTES:

_____

_____

_____

_____

_____

_____

_____

_____

_____

_____

_____

_____

_____

_____

Chapter

1

The Reality of Costs

"**M**inor cuts and bruises are part of the business—I don't have time to address all of them." Take this approach to handling safety issues and your company will lose money. Although most companies recognize the direct costs associated with safety failures, they ignore the more substantial indirect costs. Furthermore, most companies consolidate their Workers' Compensation Insurance costs at the highest level of the organization. Few middle managers realize the financial effects that safety failures have on their bottom line.

The Cost of Workers' Comp

By state law, your company is required to maintain Workers' Compensation Insurance. This insurance covers your employees' medical expenses and compensates them for missed work or loss of ability. The insurance is purchased on the open market from insurance companies in the same manner as car insurance. As with car insurance, the higher the deductible, the lower the premiums. Most large companies, therefore, hold policies with an extremely high deductible (up to $500,000 per claim) to keep the premiums low. When an employee files a claim, all of the money (in California, up to $728 per week in salary alone) comes off of the company's bottom line until the deductible is reached. In most cases, the deductible amount is never reached; in effect making the company cover its own Workers Compensation Insurance. Furthermore, Workers' Compensation Insurance premiums have jumped significantly in recent years due to a number of carriers leaving the marketplace. High deductibles, rising premiums—Workers' Compensation Insurance is expensive.

What is your company's deductible for Workers' Compensation Insurance?

The True Costs of Safety Failures

Even if your Workers' Compensation Insurance premium is low and the deductible is zero, these costs are just the beginning of safety failure expenses. Based on a three-year review of occupational injuries for a multi-national industrial services company, we concluded that costs covered by Workers' Compensation Insurance are just a small part of the true costs of safety failures. The study evaluated not only the direct costs of workplace injuries and illnesses, such as medical expenses and employee compensation, but indirect costs, such as loss in productivity, loss in morale, retraining, and management time to analyze and address issues. The study determined that injuries requiring basic first-aid treatment cost a company an average of $6,000 per incident. A non-loss time injury (that is an injury where the employee can return to work for his/her next scheduled shift) cost the employer an average $13,000. If an employee cannot complete any or all parts of his/her normal assignment during subsequent workdays or shifts, the injury is a loss-time injury (LTI). A company's bottom-line losses average $30,000 for a minor LTI and the costs can potentially reach into the hundreds of thousands in more severe cases.

NOTE: Later in this chapter you will work though the actual costs, both direct and indirect, associated with a workplace injury. Since this exercise takes time and research to complete for every incident, we use average numbers based on years of incident reviews for comparison purposes. To some, these numbers ($6,000 for a first aid case, $13,000 for a medical case, and $30,000 for a loss time case) seem excessively high. How can a simple first aid cost $6,000? The answer is actually quite simple and explained in depth in Chapter 5. In a nutshell, one incorrect assumption often made by employees and managers alike is the correlation between injury severity and the cost of the injury. If an organization is properly addressing safety issues, the funds spent on the analysis and eventual corrective actions should be based on the potential severity and frequency, not the actual severity only. For example, an employee was hit with a glancing blow from a hook falling from an overhead hoist. Mere inches were the difference between a first aid and a fatality. The actual severity (first aid) means we were just lucky this time. Although the incident was classified as first aid treatment only, the analysis and corrective actions required $100,000 in engineering work. The existing hoist system required complete retrofitting in order to both meet operational needs and eliminate the high potential for recurrence. The organization would have to experience more than fifteen additional first aid cases at zero cost in order to bring the average down to $6,000 per first aid case. Dispelling this assumption is one of the first steps in moving from chance management to logical leadership.

The Reality of Costs

To further support these averages, a recent Liberty Mutual Insurance[3] survey of top executives exposed the true costs of safety. Forty percent of the executives reported that for every $1 of direct safety costs, they spent $3 to $5 dollars in indirect costs.

How much does safety cost? Consider Company ABC with 12,000 employees. In one year, they had just over 1,000 incident reports. Based on historical data, these incidents resulted in an average Workers' Compensation cost of about $2,500 per claim. Since Company ABC carries a deductible of $250,000 it paid all of its own Workers Compensation costs. Thus in direct costs alone, this company spent over $2.5 million that year on safety failures. However, by applying the average values from above to the types of injuries suffered, this company actually lost over $8.3 million dollars in addition to any Workers' Compensation Insurance premiums.

---

[3] Cal-OSHA Reporter (10-12-2001)

Safety Costs for Company ABC

First-aid treatment: 741   X $6,000   = $4,446,000

Medical treatment
(no lost time):   243   X $13,000   = $3,159,000

LTI: 24   X $30,000   = $720,000

Total True Costs for Safety Failures: $ 8,325,000

Does it make sense? Using the following worksheet, calculate what your last employee injury really cost you.

How much does an injury cost your company?

For each of the categories, enter the total cost to your organization.

Fully loaded salary of the injured employee for any hours paid after the incident. (e.g., wage continuation) $ _____

Workers' Compensation benefits paid to the employee $ _____

Medical fees associated with the injury $ _____

Fully loaded salary of the supervisor for hours spent responding to the incident, obtaining medical assistance for employee, completing required paperwork, conducting incident analysis, developing and implementing corrective actions, counseling current employees, and interviewing, hiring, and training replacement employee $ _____

Fully loaded salary of the management team
for hours spent responding to the incident,
supporting incident analysis, reviewing
corrective actions, and dealing with regulatory
agency and customer issues arising from the
incident $ _____

Fully loaded salary for administrative support
needed to ensure the proper completion of all
forms, to work with the Workers'
Compensation Insurance to manage the claim,
and to pay invoices for costs under the
deductible $ _____

Repair or replacement of damaged equipment
or property $ _____

Implementation of engineering,
administrative, or personal protection controls   _____

Loss in productivity due to incident $ _____

Loss in sales or customers due to incident $ _____

Overtime to cover missed shifts $ _____

Total $ _____

How much money did you really lose last year to safety failures?

Record the total number of incidents[4] in the following categories:

First-aid treatment: _____ X $6,000   = $ _____

Medical treatment
(no lost time): _____ X $13,000   = $ _____

LTI: _____ X $30,000   = $ _____

Total True Costs for Safety Failures: $ _____

---

[4] If you do not have records of any occupational injuries, either your organization is unique and very safe, or it has no safety process and is significantly losing money.

Pushing Down the Liabilities

Push safety liability costs down to the lowest level possible.

Companies usually treat their Workers' Compensation Insurance costs like all other insurance costs: consolidated at the highest level of the organization. Most companies add Workers' Compensation premiums and projected claim payments, divide the total by the number of employees, and determine a rate per employee that is pushed down to the operating level. This simple method reduces management costs and duplication, and each operating group pays its fair share of overall costs based on the number of employees. Unfortunately, there is nothing "fair" about this method. It does not push the "pain" (the direct costs) back to the operating group or manager with the problem in the first place. Therefore, the manager is neither accountable nor responsible for safety failures.

> **Is your accounting system rewarding unsafe behavior?**

In fact, managing Workers' Compensation costs in this manner may actually contribute to safety failures. Compare two managers running similar operating locations for the same company. A compensation plan provides each manager with a substantial year-end bonus for his group's profitability. Greg cuts corners, takes undue risks, and tells his employees to get the job done regardless of safety. He considers safety meetings a "waste of time," and training takes a back seat. His group has several injuries over the year, but in the end, the bottom line is in the black. John is a true leader, building relationships with his employees and creating a workplace environment that promotes productivity, safety, and quality. Due to his efforts, his group has no injuries and the bottom line is also in the black, although to a lesser degree than his colleague's. Both managers receive bonuses. Greg's larger bonus in effect rewards his poor safety leadership. However, because of his behavior, the new fiscal year sees higher Workers' Compensation costs due to increased premiums and claims paid. Recognizing the potential effects on next year's bonus, Greg continues cutting corners, maybe taking even greater risks. John, on the other hand, is being punished for creating a safe workplace. His safety efforts came off his bottom line and directly reduced his bonus. Now, he must also carry the additional burden created by another manager's short sightedness. What will he do next year?

Direct safety costs should be pushed down as far as the accounting system will allow. If your company works on a project basis, any direct costs should come from the bottom line of that project. Pushing down safety costs reveals the true profitability of an operating group or individual project and gives a solid base for accurate business decisions. Pushing safety costs also forces each supervisor to carry the costs of his/her day-to-day decisions. This accountability creates a sense of responsibility at the frontline management level. This, in turn, results in a work environment that balances productivity, safety, and quality. In such a culture, your company, your clients, and your employees reap the benefits.

Summary: Chapter 1

 Myths:

- o A manager doesn't have time to deal with minor injuries.

- o Our insurance covers the costs of occupational injuries.

 Truths:

- o Occupational injuries cost you more than you think.

- o Workers' Compensation Insurance costs continue to rise.

- o Injury costs come straight from the bottom line.

Answers:

- o Educate your front-line managers by having them calculate the true costs of a safety failure.

- o Create accountability by pushing down the costs of safety failures as far as your system allows.

- o Adjust your incentive programs to reflect overall, sustainable success in all aspects of your business.

NOTES:

_____

_____

_____

_____

_____

_____

_____

_____

_____

_____

_____

_____

_____

_____

Chapter

2

The Reality of Accidents

W hat do you do when an ant zigzags across your path? You might ignore it or you might squash it.

If you consider, however, that ants don't live alone and don't travel far from their hill, you will realize that although you saw only one ant, it's not the only one around. If you found one today, you will probably find more tomorrow. You can ignore them or squash them one-by-one as they come along, but unless you eliminate the anthill, the whole colony will eventually invade your house.

The Anthill of Unsafe Behaviors

To reduce injuries, reduce unsafe behaviors by following some simple steps.

Unsafe behaviors, like ants, are usually ignored unless they result in injuries. (Even behaviors that result in minor injuries are often overlooked.) Until employees' unsafe behaviors create financial pain, such as increasing Workers'

Compensation premiums, most business leaders don't react. Once the business feels a financial impact, the question arises: "Why are we suddenly having so many accidents?" The answer is simple. The anthill appeared a long time ago—now the ants are invading.

Accident or Incident?

The word **accident** comes from the Latin *accidens* meaning "unessential quality, chance."

According to Webster's Dictionary, an **incident** is "an action likely to lead to grave consequences."

Contrary to popular belief, accidents don't happen. In fact, using the term *accident* as part of your safety program (for example, *Accident* Report or *Accident* Investigation) may send the wrong message to your employees. Safety failures occur because an unsafe behavior results in an injury. And unsafe behaviors are no accident.

Most organizations can prevent future injuries by addressing the unsafe behaviors already present. But you can't wait for

---

unsafe behaviors to come to you in the form of injury. To find the anthill, you must follow the trail of ants.

Identify Which Trail to Follow

In most organizations, several anthills flourish. You can't tackle them all at once. Instead, address only one unsafe behavior at a time. To choose a behavior, use the "SOAR" criteria. First, the behavior must be **specific**. Ambiguity in identifying the desired behavior leads to employee confusion.

SPECIFIC
OBJECTIVE
APPARENT
REPEATABLE

Instead of a "laundry list" of combined behaviors, choose one clear and concise behavior. For example, if the improper use of personal protective equipment is a problem, address a specific type of equipment (such as safety glasses). Next, the behavior must be completely **objective**. Ensure that your employees clearly understand the behavior and

Making It Work
In the beginning, focus on an unsafe behavior that is obvious and frequent. Your task will be easier and you can use the early success as a building block.

when it must be exhibited. You cannot have any ambiguity as to whether the behavior is occurring. Third, the desired behavior must be **apparent.** Tangible progress motivates people to change. If the behavior is not obvious, employees will not see the progress and will not be motivated. Finally, the behavior must be **repeatable**. Choosing an unsafe behavior that occurs only once a month, no matter how dangerous, will not allow you to measure and encourage progress.

 **List three unsafe behaviors you have seen your employees exhibit.[5]**

1. _____

2. _____

3. _____

---

[5] If you can't think of any unsafe behaviors, take a job walk or site walk. Look for the lack of personal protective equipment (safety glasses, safety shoes, gloves, and so on) or the improper use of equipment (such as ladders, power tools, and vehicles).

Measure the Success Rate

Once you have identified the behavior, you must measure it to show progress and stimulate future change. To maintain the focus, track the behavior once a day (or more often, if you prefer).

> ### Making It Work
> # Shout your appreciation.
> Whisper your corrections.

Conducting measurements is easy. Anytime you walk through the work area, focus on the SOAR behavior. When you observe the behavior, recognize that success. If an employee is not exhibiting the behavior, quietly and privately correct him/her. On the *Get the Facts* score sheet (at the end of this chapter), tally the number of observations, both successes and opportunities for improvement. After two weeks of observations, calculate a baseline success rate and communicate it to your

> ### Making It Work
> Vary the time of day you make observations. If you become predictable, employees will adjust their behaviors to your schedule.

employees. Then continue to measure, emphasize, and, if necessary, correct. Every two weeks, calculate the success rate, chart your progress, and communicate the results to your employees. This consistency will show them you are serious about improving behaviors and create an expectation on their part. Continue this cycle until your success rate stays at 100% for eight straight weeks.

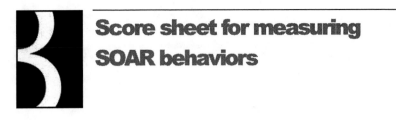

Score sheet for measuring SOAR behaviors

SOAR Behavior: _____

Date	Successes	Opportunities
_____	_____	_____
_____	_____	_____
_____	_____	_____
_____	_____	_____
_____	_____	_____
Totals:	_____	_____
	Successes	Opportunities

Success
Rate:　(_____ / _____) = _____
　　　　　　Total　　　　Total
　　　　　Successes　　Observations
　　　　　　　　　　　(Successes +
　　　　　　　　　　　Opportunities)

Reward Success

You have now successfully changed a behavior and started creating a culture. Celebrate the success. The celebration does not have to be elaborate, but it must connect the reward to the change in behavior, truly reward all employees involved, and build momentum for future changes. Use the following guidelines to plan the celebration.

- **When and Where**

  o Conduct the celebration as soon as possible upon achieving the goal.

  o Conduct the celebration at the same time and place that you usually present the progress reports.

- **What**

  o Ask the employees how they want to celebrate—don't assume you know what is important to them.

  o Be sensitive to the gender mix if giving a small gift.

o If possible, connect the reward with the behavior. (e.g., new protective glasses if the measured behavior was wearing your protective glasses).

- **Who**

  o Ensure that the celebration equally rewards everyone involved in the improvement, regardless of position or title.

  o Stay away from games or lotteries that result in a few big winners. These strategies result in a few really happy employees and many unmotivated, disappointed employees.

After the celebration, choose another behavior and start again. Once you succeed with the obvious behaviors, examine your incident history to determine behaviors that have historically resulted in frequent or severe injuries. Even better, ask your employees which behavior to target next. Over time, you will track even remote, less obvious ants and eliminate many costly anthills.

Summary: Chapter 2

 Myths:

- o Accidents happen.

- o Safety audits will keep employees safe.

- o Everyone wants a jacket with the company logo on it.

 Truths:

- o Incidents don't just "happen". The unsafe behavior has been around for a while.

- o Safety audits usually identify unsafe conditions and poorly written programs, but rarely address unsafe behaviors.

- o Not all employees are motivated by the same rewards.

Answers:

- o Focus on changing one specific behavior at a time.

- o Communicate the progress: information is a great motivator.

- o Ensure that the rewards fit the behavior and motivate the employees.

NOTES:

_____

_____

_____

_____

_____

_____

_____

_____

_____

_____

_____

_____

_____

_____

_____

Chapter

3

The Reality of Statistics

S tatistics are a double-edged sword. You can easily create statistics from any specific, objective, apparent, and repeatable action. Unfortunately, if you measure the wrong action or emphasize certain statistics too much, you will probably make poor decisions. The federal Occupational Safety and Health Administration's (Fed-OSHA) method of measuring safety success in the workplace errs in both ways, leading many companies to work at managing statistics and regulations rather than preventing injuries. To make good decisions, you need to use statistics properly. You need to measure the correct data and emphasize the right statistics.

Measure the Correct Data

OSHA Recordable Injury and Illness Rates

If they evaluate safety statistics at all, most organizations track only their OSHA Recordable Injury and Illness Rate (RIIR), which is based on the number of recordable[6] injuries expected annually for every 100 full-time employees. Many organizations, including Fed-OSHA, use the RIIR to evaluate a company's overall safety performance. Even though the RIIR is useful for comparing organizations in similar fields, the statistic itself does nothing to reduce safety failures.

 **What is the average RIIR for your industry?[7]**

Since companies calculate their own RIIRs, they usually determine the most favorable rate. By calculating the RIIR at the highest level in the organization (and therefore including administrative and management hours), a company can

[6] The recordability of an injury or illness can be determined using "Recordkeeping Guidelines for Occupational Injuries and Illness" published by the U.S. Department of Labor.

[7] To find the most recent RIIRs by industry, go to the United States Bureau of Labor Statistics web site (http://data.bls.gov/labjava/outside.jsp?survey=sh).

significantly lower its rate. Unfortunately, although looking at safety from 30,000 feet up gives the company a nice view, it does not accurately represent safety performance nor provide the data necessary to make smart decisions and protect profits.

What is your organization's RIIR?

(No. of Recordable Injuries or Illnesses)

x 200,000

―――――――――――――――――――――   =   ―――――

Number of hours worked[8]

Even if the RIIR were pushed down to the supervisor level, it would not truly evaluate the safety of that supervisor and team. Most companies have so few OSHA recordable injuries and

---

[8] The total number of hours worked can occur within any time frame, but most RIIRs are calculated on an annual basis.

illnesses that a vast majority of supervisors would have an RIIR of zero, while the remaining few would have RIIRs in the triple digits. Evaluating supervisors in this way would be like evaluating a baseball manager on the rate of failed sacrifice bunts per game. Neither recordable injuries nor sacrifice bunts happen often enough to truly measure performance. Furthermore, luck and manageability influences the number of recordable injuries. To stay with the baseball analogy, sometimes luck determines whether a manager calls for a sacrifice bunt. If, by luck, a manager never encounters that situation, the players will never fail. As for manageability, how many managers who were being evaluated on sacrifice bunts would ask a player to attempt one? Winning or losing would become irrelevant as long as no sacrifice bunts failed. In the same way, with luck or aggressive incident management, supervisors with zero RIIRs would be rated "safe," even though they could be moments away from triple digits.

Creating Useful Safety Statistics

Statistics are only useful if they motivate improvement. Since people are motivated by challenges, the bigger the safety statistic, the better. After all, if your company had an RIIR of 1.00, how hard would you work towards 0.95? Most organizations would rather focus on other issues, noticing safety only when the number increased. To create a statistic that will motivate and provide a realistic picture, the measurable action must occur frequently. Luck and manageability must be controlled. The Total Injury and Illness Rate (TIIR) achieves both goals.

The TIIR uses the same formula as the RIIR, but it measures the number of incidents resulting in (at least) first aid treatment. This statistic more accurately evaluates safe behavior. The measurable action occurs more frequently and on a more basic level than the RIIR action, minimizing the elements of luck. And, unlike the RIIR, the company cannot make the first aid incident disappear by managing the post-incident activities. The TIIR is also more motivating: the number is bigger, leaving more room for significant improvement.

Consider two operating locations from the same company that offer similar services to similar industries. The groups are of similar size and report into the same senior management structure.

	Hawaii	Salt Lake
• **Hours Worked**	122,621	125,427
• **Recordable Incidents**	5	1
• **OSHA RIIR**	8.16	1.59

According to the RIIR, the Salt Lake City location appears to be the safer operation. In fact, the company incentive program rewarded Salt Lake City's management team for its safety performance. However, evaluating the locations with the TIIR changes the picture.

	Hawaii	Salt Lake
• **Hours Worked**	122,621	125,427
• **Recordable Incidents**	5	1
• **OSHA RIIR**	8.16	1.59
• **Total Incidents**	8	12
• **TIIR**	13.05	19.13

According to the new statistics, the Hawaii location is actually safer. Where would you distribute incentive awards now?

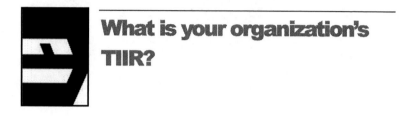

What is your organization's TIIR?

$$\frac{(\text{No. of Injuries or Illnesses}) \times 200{,}000}{\text{Number of hours worked}[9]} \quad = \quad \underline{\hspace{2cm}}$$

---

[9] The total number of hours worked can occur within any time frame, but most RIIRs use a year.

Track the Correct Statistics: Who

Use statistics properly to track two "whos."

Unfortunately, even the TIIR indicates past performance, not future potential. One way to prevent future safety failures is to find a pattern in the past. To find a pattern, you must track safety incidents.

Few companies take the time and effort to investigate incidents and generate investigation reports, let alone track the data collected. Those organizations that actually track the information usually record only types of injuries, body part affected, or time of day. These statistics can provide important information, but are usually of little use unless the sample size is large enough to reveal trends. Regardless of how you define an incident or at what level you track it, the real key is to track the "who," not the what.

Tracking "who" is important on two levels. The first "who" is the individual having the incident. Interviews with hundreds of managers indicate that employees with continual safety problems are most often the employees with continual performance problems. Whether repetitive safety failures affect the employee's performance or the employee's performance issues create safety failures is unclear. Either way, you cannot risk the continued employment of individuals with safety or performance issues. Protect yourself, protect your profits, and protect that employee by removing him/her from your organization.

Tracking the second "who"—the direct supervisors of the employees having incidents— is even more important. Supervisors dictate the work environment. A good supervisor leads by example and creates an atmosphere where motivated individuals succeed. A poor supervisor manages by edict, fear, and confusion—a breeding ground for unsafe and costly behaviors. Resolve the supervisor problems, and you will minimize greater troubles in the future.

The "Who's Who" of Injuries

List the names of your front-line management team. Using the formulas for RIIR and TIIR above, calculate each value based on the employees/projects for which each supervisor has responsibility.

Name	RIIR	TIIR

Summary: Chapter 3

 Myths:

- o A low OSHA RIIR means a safe workplace.

- o The OSHA RIIR is a true measure of the organization's commitment to safety.

Truths:

- o The OSHA RIIR does not measure severity and can be easily manipulated.

- o Luck plays a huge role in an organization's OSHA RIIR.

- o Although still a measure of failure, the TIIR gives a truer picture of the organization's safety performance.

Answers:

- o Use the TIIR and other statistics to remove luck and manageability from the numbers.

- o Calculate the statistics as low as possible to expose problem areas and people.

- o Track the two "whos" and make better business decisions.

NOTES:

_____

_____

_____

_____

_____

_____

_____

_____

_____

_____

_____

_____

_____

_____

Chapter

4

The Reality of Regulations

W hen you drive down the highway, do you drive the speed limit? If you have a driver's license, you have been trained, tested, and evaluated on the proper operation of a motor vehicle and the rules of the road. Those same rules are plainly and frequently posted for everyone to see, and conspicuous safety coordinators (aka "highway patrol" or "state troopers") remind you to follow them. If you drive enough, you have probably been issued a ticket or have seen a severe, maybe even fatal, incident. So if drivers know the rules of the road and have experienced the pain associated with violating them, why do they speed? Just as the speed limit doesn't guarantee that all people will drive safely, enforcing OSHA's regulations will not stop your employees from taking risks.

Why Compliance Is Mandatory

Even though regulations will not protect your employees, the minimum level of compliance is mandatory to defend your profits. Every business in the United States must comply with the U.S. Occupational Safety and Health (Fed OSHA) regulations codified in 29 CFR, either the General Industry requirements of 29 CFR 1910 or the Construction Industry requirements of 29 CFR 1926. In addition to the federal requirements, twenty-six states run their own OSHA programs. Each of these states has developed additional regulations applicable to varying degrees (although their specific regulations must be at least as stringent as the federal requirements).

Have federal or state OSHA inspectors visited your facility recently?

Date of Inspection	Reason for Inspection	Notice of Violation Issued	Fines Levied
_____	_____	_____	_____
_____	_____	_____	_____
_____	_____	_____	_____
_____	_____	_____	_____

Like police officers on traffic patrol, OSHA inspectors enforce the regulations. OSHA inspectors, whether on the state or federal level, visit facilities for one of four reasons: to respond to severe or multiple injuries, to respond to employee complaints, to conduct targeted inspections[10], or to conduct random inspections. Based on historical information and current events, you are unlikely to experience a random or targeted inspection. However, if an incident requires reporting to OSHA or an employee complains, OSHA will investigate. And when inspectors show up at your facility, they will find a violation. If the violations are severe or willful, you have not only failed to defend your profits, you may need a lawyer to defend your freedom. Therefore, regardless of your organization's location, you must comply with the federal and state regulations. However, creating a world-class compliance program may do little to keep your employees safe.

OSHA Can't Protect Your Employees[11]

In the last thirty years, Fed OSHA has written rules and regulations to protect employees—with some success. Over the past 25 years, the OSHA Recordable Injury and Illness Rate (RIIR) for private industry has declined almost 30% (9.3 to 6.3), an average of 1.4% per year.

---

[10] Based on statistics from previous years, OSHA will target certain industries for more frequent inspections.

[11] All statistics obtained from the U.S. Bureau of Labor Statistics, 2002.

This progress seems impressive until you consider a couple of factors. First, during this 25-year period, 14% of the U.S. workforce moved from the manufacturing sector (with a 1999 RIIR of 9.2) to the services sector (1999 RIIR of 4.9). That is, 14% of the U.S. workforce moved to a substantially safer work environment, making OSHA's job much easier. Second, when the OSHA RIIR gets smaller, improvement becomes tougher. Over the same 25 years, the two "safest" sectors, the finance/insurance/real estate sector and the services sector, saw minimal reductions of 10% (2.0 to 1.8) and 7.5% (5.3 to 4.9), respectively. Finally, since OSHA has had thirty years to write these rules, why isn't everyone always safe? If regulations changed behaviors, shouldn't the OSHA RIIR now be zero?

Safety rules and regulations do not stop all employees from taking all risks. (After all, how many people drive the speed limit all the time?) No matter how detailed the rules, how well-documented the procedures, how frequently communicated the issues, how stringent the penalties, factors other than rules and regulations encourage employees to take unnecessary risks.

Spend Your Resources Wisely

You have limited resources, so do you want compliance or commitment?

Every organization has limited resources to commit to any portion of their business, including safety. How should you spend those resources? If your employees are getting hurt and your Workers' Compensation costs are soaring, updating your written hazard communication program is not important. Yet when auditors and inspectors visit facilities, they look for such regulatory violations. So should you spend money maintaining compliance or creating commitment?

Where did you spend your resources last year?

Enter the total number of dollars spent in each category:

OSHA

Fines

True Cost

of Safety

Failures[12]

---

[12] Refer to the Quick Check in Chapter 1.

Most businesses spend their safety prevention money in four areas: written programs, training, audits, and employee incentives. The rest of this chapter shows how to comply with OSHA requirements without spending all your money[13].

Written Programs

The major OSHA regulations require you to write a program to outline your compliance methods. Usually, you must review the written programs annually. OSHA's regulations provide minimum requirements, but you can make these written programs as simple or as complex as you desire. Unless you're seeking some type of certification, do not strive for world-class documents. Most trade associations offer template documents to their membership. Use these templates to create your written programs quickly and completely. As for updates, unless your business has changed, read through the program to ensure the elements are still accurate, place a new date on the forms, and file them away for another year. Remember, many tremendous safety manuals collect dust on the shelf while the manager sends another employee to the doctor. Other very safe organizations wouldn't know an OSHA 300 log from a cheese log.

---

[13] Chapter 5 presents tools for creating a safe workplace.

Training

Training costs time and money. The costs of the instructor's time, the employees' time, and most importantly, the loss in productivity, makes training very expensive. Therefore, most organizations conduct <u>safety</u> training because OSHA requires it. So we look for a way to provide the required content in the fastest and cheapest method that allows for easy documentation to demonstrate compliance. Based on this philosophy, we tend to generalize and compartmentalize our safety training based on the regulation introducing the employees to the required elements and concepts.

If your goal is fast, cheap and easily documented, generic on-line programs are the way to go. These programs can be used to introduce the required elements and concepts with questions or company-specific issues handled one-on-one with the employee and their supervisor. In addition, many on-line training companies even offer learning management systems to track training completion, giving you even better compliance documentation.

However, as with any training, the tools and concepts are useful only if reinforced in the real world. Generic on-line programs can not give you employees this support. Our goal must be to move past compliance documentation toward actually integrating safety as part of the work process. The safety elements of the work process need to be taught at the same time and by the same person that teaches the productivity and quality elements: the supervisor. To further support the implementation of the safety information, your supervisors must Expect, Exhibit, and Emphasize the safe work habits (see "E-Safety" Chapter 5). This approach has two main benefits. The first is that the supervisor is conveying a balanced message of safety, productivity and quality by taking ownership of the entire work process. The second is, with a little extra effort, the supervisor can document the communication significantly reducing the direct and indirect costs associated with classroom training.

Audits

Auditors and inspectors often review documents, comb through training records, and walk around an operation listing all the things that are wrong. This broad approach can establish a baseline—the information you need to begin to address safety issues. Usually, however, these broad-based audits result in a lengthy list of problems that you try to fix for the next six months. Unfortunately, unless you change behaviors, these problems become "unfixed" as soon as you walk away. Instead of wasting resources on broad scope monthly or annual audits, use the focused approach described in Chapter 2 (SOAR) to promote true change and continual improvement.

Incentive Programs

Employees will focus on whatever gets them rewarded. Safety incentive programs may increase safety awareness, for a while. However, incentive programs geared solely to safety have significant problems. First, employees decide to take a risk instantaneously, not after contemplating the effects on a safety incentive to be awarded next month. Second, for rewards based on individual performance, a safety incentive program discourages employees from looking out for co-workers and promotes the "hiding" of incidents. If the program is based on a team effort and someone gets injured, the safe employees are still penalized. Therefore, base any incentive program you implement on the employee's ability to meet short-term goals, incorporating all elements of success (safety, quality, and productivity). This type of program not only provides motivation, it also educates your employees on the balance necessary to achieve organizational success.

Safety Committees

Traditional employee safety committees, sometimes overseen by a management steering committee, are chartered to address safety issues, investigate accidents, develop safety incentive programs, and participate in observations and audits. However, there are several inherent flaws in the structure of the standard safety committee. These flaws almost always render a group ineffective over time, and essentially reduce them to well-meaning participants in a monthly pizza gathering on the company's dime.

- **Participants**

  o Most safety committees are comprised of volunteers…or those who have been volunteered. Either way, we get a group of individuals whom we may not have selected to address a particular concern. Although these types of participants may bring 'a new set of eyes' to an issue, unless they have a vested interest in accomplishing the goal, they may not bring the value and buy-in needed. In addition, they very well may lack the technical expertise to efficiently resolve the issue.

- **Size**

  o Often, the desire of the management team is to have each department or work group represented on the committee. Unfortunately, this creates a large committee which has a difficult time staying organized and on task let alone reaching consensus.

- **Time**

  o Many organizations mandate that their safety committees meet monthly for a specific period of time, commonly one year. At the end of the year's time, the members are rotated out with new employees brought on board. The idea being that by rotating members, the committee will become a vehicle to spread safety ownership. Unfortunately, this model creates both short-term and long-term problems. Since the committee is often quite large, bringing them all together for an impromptu meeting is virtually impossible. Therefore, progress stalls until the next regularly scheduled monthly meeting. In the long-term, with finite time frames and rotating members, the committee is often slowed or stalled, reinventing the wheel each time there is membership change. If a committee has begun an initiative, it now becomes the responsibility of the new members to carry on the initiative with the same passion even if it is not a priority for them. When the initiative fails due to lack of support, it is seen by the employees as a 'program of the month' damaging the success potential of future initiatives.

- **Goal and Measurable Results**

  o The success of an ergonomic improvement is easily measured through time and weight studies. However, measuring the effectiveness of other safety resolutions creates a more difficult challenge. Many safety committees see their job as reducing injury rates or workers' compensation costs. However, these traditional safety measures are driven by many variables and external influences. An attempt to track changes in these measures directly back to the committee's activities would be tenuous at best. Therefore, the success of a safety committee is almost impossible to measure.

- **Authority**

  o Many safety committee members find themselves in the position of 'safety cops' wearing their 'safety' shirt and trying to identify and correct compliance and behavioral issues. For those members that are overzealous, this can become an issue with their co-workers and cause riffs within the team. For those members who were volunteered, this added responsibility becomes a burden and a nuisance.

- **Abdication**

  o Committee members often become the eyes and ears of the safety department. As such, the members become the 'safety person' for their department or work group, allowing the supervisor to abdicate his or her responsibility in this area. This perpetuates the impression that supervisors are responsible for productivity and the safety department and the safety committee are responsible for safety. To further this point, we have to ask, "Who is on the productivity committee?" The answer, obviously, is the supervisors. So, the supervisors are responsible for productivity, and a group of random employees is responsible for safety? By creating a standing safety committee, we are allowing supervisors to abdicate their responsibilities for creating a balanced work environment.

If you are required to have a safety committee, the key is to maximize the use of these resources without undermining the supervisor's responsibility. One possible approach is to form small task-specific teams (you can call them a "safety committee" if you need to) to address a very specific safety-related issue. By having these task-specific teams, we resolve many of the challenges that most traditional standing safety committees face.

- **Participants**

  o By choosing a small team with the expertise and the interest, we can get better results that will be more readily accepted. Employees will better support a world which they create.

- **Size**

  o The size of the team can be limited to those with the expertise, knowledge, and ability to resolve the issue. This makes for a focused results-driven team that can get together as frequently as needed.

- **Time**

  o Since these teams are convened to address a single issue, the time-frame to resolve the issue should be established by the team and approved by the senior management. Due to the relatively small size of the team, quick, impromptu meetings are easily organized and completed allowing the project to move forward quickly. Once the issue is resolved, the team is disbanded and a new process begins.

- **Goal and Measurable Results**

  o By forming task-specific teams, the goal and the measure are inherently identified during the formation of the team. This format allows for managers to easily track the success of the team and their activities. With specific goals and measurable results, members will be motivated to join future teams once they have experienced the success of their task-force.

- **Authority**

  o Task-specific teams will not get drawn into the position of 'safety cop' since identification of issues is not their charter. Their task is to identify the engineering, administrative, and personal protective controls necessary to address the issue. The responsibility for the implementation of the changes then falls back where it belongs: on the supervisor.

- **Abdication**

    o   Task-specific teams will not have the scope of
        responsibility to allow for this abdication.
        The overall responsibility for success remains
        with the supervisor.

By maintaining compliance in a cost-effective manner, you can
then spend your resources effectively to create commitment.
Remember, OSHA compliance does not necessarily mean a
safe work environment. To be successful, your commitment to
safety must go beyond the regulations.

Safety Committees vs. Task-Specific Teams

		Safety Committees		Task-Specific Teams
Participants		By Department		By Skill Set
Size		Large and Unwieldy		Small and targeted
Time		Calendar-based		Resolution-based
Goal and Measurable Results		Unpredictable and ambiguous		Focused and clearly defined
Authority		None		Complete
Supervisor's Abdication		Total		Limited to scope

Summary: Chapter 4

 Myths:

- o OSHA compliance means a safe workplace.

- o Once employees are trained on the rules, they will be safe.

- o OSHA fines are huge.

Truths:

- o Most people disregard the rules if they don't perceive a risk.

- o OSHA compliance is mandatory to defend your profits and your freedom.

- o OSHA compliance alone will not protect your employees or defend your profits.

Answers:

- o Integrate the safety elements into supervisor-led work process training that covers productivity and quality.

- o Use incentive programs that promote overall business success.

- o Use small task-specific teams to address specific issues.

NOTES:

_____

_____

_____

_____

_____

_____

_____

_____

_____

_____

_____

_____

_____

_____

_____

Chapter

5

The Reality of Culture

A
n inherent flaw in the way many of us approach improvement is that our level of interest in a particular situation is based on the actual results of our actions. As found in many organizations and throughout society, our level of interest is tied more frequently to the actual results of an action, instead of the potential results. This starts all the way back in youth athletics, when a five-year old soccer player "hogs" the ball. Time and again they ignore open teammates and fail to pass the ball. However, with some determination and a lot of luck, they eventually score a goal. After a goal, the parents cheer, the teammates jump up and down, and the player is provided positive consequences for obtaining a single result that in fact is detrimental to the overall success of the team and the development of that player. We can also see this flawed correlation in the way we deal with criminals. Grand theft brings a stiffer penalty than petty theft. The same event, the same intent, a different result draws a different consequence. Unfortunately, we bring this same approach to the workplace when dealing with injuries.

Severity-Based Safety

In many organizations, politics dictate the level of response for safety incidents based on the actual severity. The more severe the injury: the more detailed and serious the organization's response. Often this is based on a trickle down effect. The corporate office gets excited with the loss of time. The operations or plant manager requires a board of review when there is an OSHA recordable injury. The supervisor may pay attention to a first aid case, but often times, they don't get too concerned until the employee needs medical treatment.

The arrows on the following diagram indicate the point on the severity continuum where the level of interest resides for a specific part of the typical management team.

Typical Management Team Focused on Actual Severity

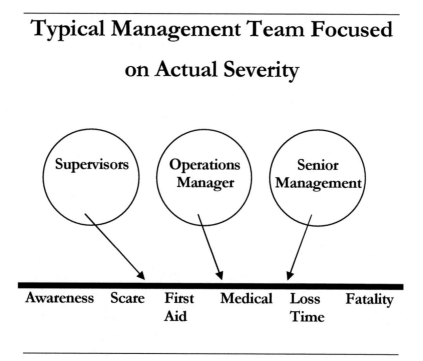

| Supervisors | Operations Manager | Senior Management |

Awareness   Scare   First Aid   Medical   Loss Time   Fatality

When Does Your Management Team Get Involved?

On the continuum of severity below, draw a line to where the senior management of your organization demands action? At what level does the operations manager get excited? At what level does the supervisor want to drive a change?

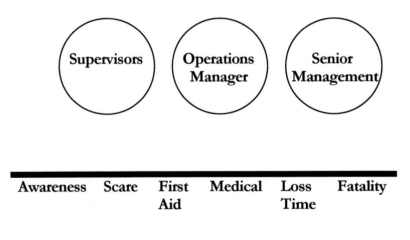

| Awareness | Scare | First Aid | Medical | Loss Time | Fatality |

Regardless as to where the lines are drawn on the continuum above, basing the level of interest on the actual severity of the injury is truly **management by luck.**

Management by Luck

One of the most common safety fallacies that supervisors and managers often fall for is this belief that the seriousness of the response must be related to the severity of the injury. For example, an employee reaches into an energized piece of equipment and receives the slightest of shocks. Two minutes later, he does the same thing and is severely electrocuted. By basing our response on the actual severity of the injury, the latter event requires a serious response while the former requires barely a mention. The severity of the injury is the only difference between the two incidents and that is solely a matter of luck. Unfortunately, traditional safety management has propagated this fallacy over the years by highlighting the actual severity by the way we categorize incidents and measure our success or failure. The simple fact that we regularly use the terms 'near miss', 'recordable injury', and 'loss time injury' drives management to this ridiculous approach. The fact that we measure an organization's success by the same criteria is absolutely absurd. This flawed approach means the bigger the injury, the more complicated and intensive the analysis and corrective actions. This philosophy, also perpetuated by other elements of traditional safety programs, results in:

- A lack of accountability and responsibility;

- A lack of credibility due to unclear expectations and inconsistent messages;

- The loss of time and money implementing costly, unnecessary and ineffective corrective actions for the sake of action itself; and,

- The loss of many opportunities for improvement.

These losses not only damage the safety culture, they can destroy the overall culture of the organization.

Lack of Accountability and Responsibility

(or "I can't believe my employee would do something so stupid!")

If the operations manager does not get involved with an issue until the actual severity reaches the OSHA recordable threshold, then she is neither accountable nor responsible for anything less. The same goes for the supervisors. If they do not respond until the employee gets hurt, they too can say that they are neither accountable nor responsible. This makes it very easy to then blame the employee, and clears the path to retraining and discipline: the most common - and easiest - corrective actions.

Lack of Credibility

(or "Management won't do anything until someone gets hurt.")

The real hypocrisy of this approach lies in the fact that we expect our employees to bring safety issues to our attention as soon as they become aware of them. However, their lessons of experience (see Chapter 6) tell them that management will only respond to an issue as the actual severity increases.

If the thought process equates actual severity with seriousness of response, our actions appear to be knee-jerk and extremely inconsistent. The inconsistency arises, as described above, because the severity of the resulting injuries is a matter of luck. Let's return to the example of the employee reaching into the energized piece of equipment, but change the scenario slightly. This time, two different employees take the very same action: each reaches into an energized piece of equipment. The first receives the slightest of shocks. The second is severely electrocuted. When the management team treats the two employees differently, the inconsistency is obvious to all. These inconsistent responses by management undermine the credibility of the safety program, the supervisory staff, and the senior management team. Employees do notice. They recognize when their supervisor says one thing and does another. This becomes even more apparent when disciplinary actions are taken against an employee who became injured for doing the same things that he has seen his supervisor do many times.

Contributing to this loss of credibility is the lack of clear expectations. When employees do not know what to expect in the way of a response, they are either disappointed or disillusioned. Employees are told that safety is important and they can always stop what they are doing if they think it is unsafe. When they do so, however, and are met with impatience or outright hostility, their trust in the integrity of the organization declines. Without clear expectations, their interpretation of 'safe' deteriorates over time to 'just don't get hurt'.

Costly, Ineffective Corrective Actions for the Sake of Action

(or "You had a loss time!!! Well, what are you going to do about it?")

Although it is true that medical costs are significantly higher for a broken bone than they are for a small cut, the big dollars associated with safety are buried in the engineering and operational changes made in the name of a safer work environment. When our responses are based on the actual severity instead of the potential severity and frequency, we become trapped into taking corrective action for the sake of taking action. Often these actions don't address the actual causes and result in costly, ineffective changes. Such changes are both financially and culturally damaging.

Missed Opportunities

(or "I just knew that someone was going to get hurt doing that!")

Statistics and anecdotal evidence tell us that we often have several, if not many, opportunities to fix a problem before someone gets seriously injured. However, a team that manages by luck misses these opportunities because they are too busy reviewing statistics, enforcing rules, and developing ineffective corrective actions.

Logic Leadership

Leadership through logic leaves nothing to chance.

Logic dictates that our response must be based on the potential severity and frequency instead of the actual severity. Your management team must take the same initial approach to a safety issue regardless of the actual severity.

When Should Your Management Team Get Involved?

Based on logic-based leadership, draw a line from each circle to the point of the severity continuum which corresponds to an appropriate level of interest.

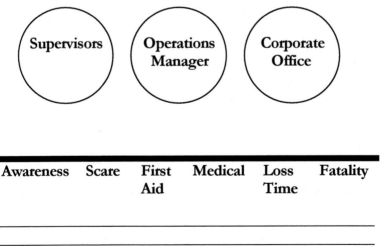

Awareness	Scare	First Aid	Medical	Loss Time	Fatality

Of course the lines are now at the far left, and consistent with our expectation of our employees. There is no place where, in good conscience, we can draw that line other than at the awareness level. This shift now drives the culture to accountability and responsibility, increased credibility, effective corrective actions, and continuous improvement.

Comparison of Results

Management By Luck	Leadership Through Logic
Abdicate Accountability and Responsibility	Accept Accountability and Responsibility
Lose Credibility Through Confusion and Inconsistencies	Build Trust Through Clear Expectations and a Consistent Approach
Take Action for the Sake of Action	Implement Effective Corrective Actions
Miss Opportunities	Constant Evaluation

Create Accountability and Responsibility

No one shows up to work hoping to get injured. From the time we wake up in the morning until we go to sleep at night, we manage our risks. We accomplish this primarily through pace (how fast we do things) and focus (how close we pay attention). Inherently, most of us know where our comfort level is with respect to pace and focus. Whether we are driving a car or using a nail gun, pace and focus are two factors that either increase or decrease our level of risk. The supervisor is primarily responsible for creating the environment wherein his employees safely produce a quality product. In this environment, employees will work hard while managing their own pace and focus. When an employee's pace and/or focus moves outside the comfort zone, they are no longer managing their risk. Comments by the supervisor such as "Hurry up, we are behind schedule!", "Aren't you finished yet?", and "I just need you to get it done!" push the employee's internal pace and focus gauges out of balance.

Supervisors who are only concerned with "pace" end up with injured employees. They have abdicated their responsibility to maintain efficient pace with appropriate focus. To increase the level of accountability and responsibility, we need to examine all of the systems and policies in place that allow and encourage the supervisor to abdicate their role. We can help supervisors better understand this new thought process by increasing their involvement after an employee is injured.

Organizations that successfully create this accountability and responsibility for safety require that the supervisor, not the safety manager, take the injured employee to the doctor. This simple move sends a strong message to the supervisor ("It is part of your job"). As an additional bonus, it tells the employee that the supervisor is truly concerned for their wellbeing. The second step in this process occurs if and when the employee returns to work with short-term limitations. Upon return, they go to work in their original department. The more effective the supervisor is in giving the employee rewarding and value-added work, the more the employee will feel part of the team and appreciated. Put yourself in the place of the injured employee. Would you rather be at home doing nothing, at work counting paperclips away from your work team, or in your work environment with your teammates contributing to the team's success? Under which circumstances do you think the employee will heal faster and return to be a productive, committed employee? The supervisor remains responsible and accountable for the success (defined as productivity, quality, and safety) of their people and their department.

Build Trust

Trust is built through clear expectations and a consistent approach. By focusing on the potential severity and frequency, employees know what to expect and know that the approach will be consistent based on the action, not the actual severity.

This is obviously a little more difficult than management by luck, but it is the only viable path. Recently, an operations manager asked, "Does this mean we have to do a big investigation with photos and a thirty-page report for every near miss?" The answer is "No". However, we must ensure that our response to everything from an idea to a fatality is consistent in our approach. After an initial review based on the potential severity and frequency, we can minimize the time spent on those issues with low potential in either severity or frequency. This will allow us to focus our limited resources on the issues that present both high severity and frequency potential. The initial review is the key.

The level of severity or frequency at which the organization takes action is up to the organization. There is no rule of thumb. One organization may be struggling to review issues that could potentially cause a fatality. Others may have the resources to fully examine the issues that present the potential for a cut finger. The injury history of your organization and industry is probably a good indicator as to where you draw the line. Regardless, the following five questions will help in developing a consistent initial approach.

- Is there a reasonable potential for:

    o   Electrocution;
    o   Suffocation;
    o   Asphyxiation;
    o   Engulfment;
    o   Poisoning;
    o   Falling from a height of more than six feet; or
    o   Having the head or entire body crushed by machinery, equipment, or elevated loads?

- Is there a reasonable potential for fire, explosion, or large chemical release?

- Is there a reasonable potential for the amputation of a limb or digit?

- Is there a reasonable potential for back, shoulder, arm or leg muscle strain?

- Is there the potential for this situation to occur:

    o   Several times each day
    o   Daily
    o   Weekly
    o   Monthly
    o   Annually; or
    o   Only once.

Once an organization has established its own definition of 'reasonable potential', full incident analyses can be conducted to determine effective corrected actions.

Effective Corrective Actions

Leading with logic allows the management team to develop and implement effective corrective actions instead of just taking action for the sake of action. Under this approach, it is acceptable to do nothing if the evaluation of the issue warrants no action. However, so that we do not ruin the trust we have build with our employees, when action is warranted, we must take action. Basing that action on logic allows us to evaluate engineering, administrative, and personal protection controls that are applicable and reasonable. In addition, logic frees us from using discipline and retraining as our fallback corrective actions because we have to "do something". If the employee knew the correct procedure or process and did not use it, then retraining is just another form of discipline. It is simply being used to disguise those situations where an employee's behavior exposes a flaw in leadership.

Employees make decisions constantly throughout the work day. When they stop managing their risks, they do it for one of three reasons: they were unaware of the proper behavior; they were physically unable to do the task properly; or they were improperly motivated to do the task properly. To develop an effective correction action, we must determine the employee's decision process.

Unaware

To determine if an employee was unaware of the proper method for completing the task, we can simply ask:

- Have you completed this task before?

- Tell me what the procedures are.

If they have not completed the task before or they do not know the correct steps, then they are unaware and we need to reevaluate the training process and retrain the employee.

Unable

To determine if an employee was physically unable to properly complete the task, we can simply ask and watch:

- Can you show me how you normally complete this task?

- Observe the employee completing the task.

If they can not physically complete the task according to standard procedure without putting themselves at risk, then they are unable and we need reevaluate a number of items: the work process, the hiring/promotion process, the job assignment process, and the employee's role within the organization.

Improperly Motivated

If the employee is aware and able, then his decision to take that action was based upon outside influences motivating his decisions. Due to something in the environment, he lost his balance of pace and focus. Find out what influence caused him to lose the balance and you can develop an applicable, effective corrective action.

Constant Evaluation

To move toward "awareness" on the left hand side of the severity continuum, the supervisor must also redefine success on a personal level. Focusing on awareness requires the supervisor to take some actions that might not always be the most obvious or the most comfortable.

Be Present

The supervisor can not possibly know what is occurring in their department if they are in the office or in another department fixing issues. Successfully balancing quality, safety, and productivity requires the supervisor to orchestrate the work flow. A single employee or department does not instantaneously get behind unless there is significant rework that needs to be completed. It takes time to fall behind. If the supervisor is in the area, observing the work flow and orchestrating his department, he can see these issues arise and make adjustments prior to anyone falling too far behind. Once we fall behind, the decision lines start to blur and the operation falls out of balance.

Be Aware

Supervisors are often promoted because they are seen as dependable hard workers. These are qualities that we hope they will then instill in their employees. However, making the switch from worker to leader is not easy for some. The self satisfaction we get from completing a task is often lost when our job requires us to think, lead, and teach, and we are no longer producing a tangible product. If the new position does not provide this sense of accomplishment, they will tend to drift back to the activities that do. In other words, they will start working instead of leading. Effective leaders do not work in the physical sense of the word. Their work must be mental. Mental work requires them to stop, observe, plan, and implement in order to maintain the balance of safety, productivity, and quality. If the supervisor is getting supplies or fixing equipment, they cannot be focused on maintaining that balance. Just being in the work area is not enough. The supervisor needs to stop working and start observing in order to achieve success.

Be Balanced

After the personal shift in mind set from 'doing' to 'leading', the next shift the supervisor needs to make is from 'individual production' to 'team production'. When a supervisor first moves into the observation mode, he starts looking at each employee's individual contribution (e.g., how fast can he get the task done). By shifting our focus to team production, we can start looking more closely at the work process and the management systems in place. We can determine which processes and systems make the team more effective, and allow us to safely produce even more high-quality products. If a new idea is rebuffed with "it sounds like too many guys to do one job", we are still focused on individual production and may be missing opportunities to improve the process. The supervisor should not be telling the employees to work faster; he should be asking them how we can work smarter. The more the supervisor can focus on the work process, the easier it becomes to balance productivity, quality and safety.

Summary: Chapter 5

 Myths:

- o The Safety Department is responsible for safety.

- o The more severe the actual injury, the higher the actual costs and the greater the need for corrective actions.

 Truths:

- o Employees are responsible for managing their risk and supervisors are responsible for helping them do that.

- o Retraining is most often just another form of discipline.

- o Success is not about safety, it's about leadership.

Answers:

- o Supervisors should stay involved when an employee is injured.

- o Maintain a consistent approach to evaluate potential severity and frequency.

- o Be present and stop working.

NOTES:

_____

_____

_____

_____

_____

_____

_____

_____

_____

_____

_____

_____

_____

Chapter

6

The Reality of Safety

T hink "safety management" and you probably think of written policies and procedures, safety training, slogans, vision statements, incentive awards, and progressive disciplinary programs. But such safety program elements will not produce an incident-free workplace. Safety must be learned. This is why this book is not about safety, it is about leadership.

Learning Safety

As with all lessons, safety can be learned through either experience or effect.

Experience

People learn through experiences when they participate in or witness an event so significant that it changes the way they think and behave. In safety, learning through experience comes from both safety training and incidents.

Most workplaces conduct some type of safety training. Many supervisors expect this safety training to keep their employees safe. However, safety training, as with all training, is just an antecedent: the action that initiates a process. Safety training is fleeting—that's why

> ## Lessons of Experience:
> **Learned, usually quickly, by participating in or witnessing an event so significant that it changes the way people think and behave.**

OSHA requires "refresher" sessions. Save money with on-line safety training for the required regulatory information, and use the cost savings to develop your supervisors into effective leaders.

Learning "experienced" through incidents is much more powerful than training. Incidents, especially severe ones, often have a sobering effect on employees. Most individuals involved in or witnessing an incident quickly change their perspective and realize their vulnerability. Unfortunately, organizations that depend on incidents to teach employees the importance of safety teach the lesson too late.

Effect

Teaching safety through experience is usually ineffective (safety training), or expensive and potentially tragic (incidents). The best way

> **Lessons of Effect:**
> **Learned, usually over time, by the reinforcement of consequences arising from a specific behavior.**

to teach safety is by effect: reinforcing, over and over, the consequences of safe and unsafe behavior. Employees will not learn safety because of a safety program goal or a higher-management edict. Employees will do what they think is important to their supervisor. Front-line supervisors alone have the regular contact and influence to make safety happen.

E-Safety

To entrench safe behaviors, supervisors must Expect, Exhibit, and Emphasize.

Supervisors face a constant myriad of demands on their time and attention. Although they cannot ignore safety, the safety process doesn't have to be overbearing. For a safety process to be successful, the supervisor must entrench safe attitudes with the three E's: Expect, Exhibit, and Emphasize.

If your supervisors successfully implement the three E's, your employees will integrate safe behaviors into their daily work.

Expect

Before new employees enter the work environment, the expectation of safe behavior must be clearly established. In most cases, new employees bring at least twenty years of engrained habits and behaviors with them to the workplace. Although some of these traits will be desirable, everyone has a few habits that will result in unsafe behaviors. Continuing with the ant analogy from Chapter 2, to keep ants out, you must eliminate their opportunities to invade in the first place. Although you will not eliminate your new employees' unsafe habits immediately, you can clearly indicate that unsafe behaviors are not welcome.

Unfortunately, in organizations where safety training is required, most supervisors depend on that training to communicate and establish the expected behaviors. However, training only introduces safe behaviors; it does not establish a culture that expects them. In fact, many supervisors see safety training as a hurdle new employees need to "get out to the way"...and then forget about. Furthermore, new employees may spend several days, if not weeks, in the work environment experiencing how things are "really done" before receiving their safety training. These factors sabotage safety training. If the supervisor does not expect safe work practices from the very beginning, any safety training will quickly be forgotten and existing unsafe behaviors will be more difficult to change.

Do you expect safety?

	YES	NO
Do you require new employees to complete all training prior to entering the work environment?	_____	_____
Do you ensure that supervisors have completed the same training and are aware of the content?	_____	_____
Do you have supervisors involved in the development and delivery of training?	_____	_____
Do you have supervisors review the training content with the employee upon completion?	_____	_____
Do you require and document a period of on-the-job training that focuses on all elements of success, including safety?	_____	_____

Exhibit

Supervisors must lead by example. Supervisors who say one thing but exhibit a different behavior send a confusing message to their employees. Employees will only exhibit desired behaviors if their supervisors consistently exhibit that behavior. The supervisor sets the standard for safety behaviors.

For supervisors to lead by example, they must understand their role as leaders. Unfortunately, many companies hire or promote individuals because they are the best at their job, they have been there the longest, or they fish with the top customer. Rarely are promotions the result of outstanding leadership skills—the skills that make supervisors successful. It hurts both the company and the employee when an individual who cannot provide leadership is given authority.

All companies have a leadership development program, formal or informal. An informal leadership development program will perpetuate the leadership styles of the past. That may be fine for some organizations, but can you afford to take that chance? Building leaders is not difficult; it just takes a commitment from the organization. Investing in supervisors and their future not only reduces safety incidents and costs, it also increases productivity and quality.

3 Who taught you how to be a leader?
Who is developing your supervisors?

Emphasize

Finally, supervisors must emphasize safe behavior. Basic behavioral science and common experience suggest that although an individual is trained, that individual will not exhibit the desired behavior unless it continues to be emphasized after the training. The emphasis must be directly related to the desired behavior. Emphasis can come in many shapes and sizes: salary, evaluation, bonus, incentives, promotions, discipline, embarrassment, and so on. However, the most powerful emphasis is simple: positive verbal feedback. The supervisor—the person with the most frequent and meaningful contact with employees—can provide this positive feedback, creating a culture of safety one person at a time.

Safety's Silver Bullet?

If a safety guarantee existed, it would be explained here. Unfortunately, no "silver bullet" will solve safety problems within an organization. Nor can safety problems be solved overnight with a new program, new slogan, or new safety manager. Business leaders who create a safe work environment have made safety just one of the critical elements of success: nothing more, nothing less.

> **Happy, healthy employees are the key to defending your profits.**

Is safety first? You decide. Use the tools outlined in this guide and compile the information already available in your organization to make your decision. With some employees, safety may need to be first. With others, you may focus on productivity. You must find what motivates and drives your employees to safely produce a quality product.

It is unlikely that a single incident or even a series of injuries will close your business, but this book is not about safety. It is about every part of your business, and like every other part of your business, if you ignore safety, it will grow like a cancer and destroy you. If you integrate safety into your business, making it no more or no less important than any other element, you will have happy, healthy employees—the key to **defending your profits**.

Summary: Chapter 6

 Myths:

- o Safety management means writing programs and procedures.

- o Employees will do what a front-line manager tells them to do.

- o SAFETY FIRST!!

 Truths:

- o Safety is just another part of doing business: nothing more and nothing less.

- o Employees will do what they think their manager thinks is important.

- o You can and must teach leadership.

 Answers:

- o Expect safety, just like you expect productivity and quality.

- o Hire and promote based on leadership skills, not on technical skills.

- o Know where you want to go and lead.

NOTES:

_____

_____

_____

_____

_____

_____

_____

_____

_____

_____

_____

_____

_____

_____

Do You Have Profit-Saving Techniques For:
- **Safety**
- **Sales**
- **Marketing**
- **Accounting**
- **Human Resources**

We would like to include them in our next book.
We'll give you full credit of course, and send you a complimentary new edition upon publication!

Write your technique(s) in the space on the back of this sheet and mail to:

Defend Your Profits
c/o BRANTA Worldwide.
2443 Fair Oaks Blvd. #329
Sacramento, CA 95825

Or, e-mail your suggestion to **Rodney@branta.com**. To ensure you get the credit you deserve, please complete and include the following:

Name: _____

Title: _____

Company: _____

Address: _____

City, State, Zip Code: _____

Phone: _____ Ext: _____

E-mail: _____

Tell Us Your Techniques: _____

_____

_____

_____

_____

_____

_____

_____

_____

_____

_____

_____

_____

_____

 Rodney Grieve is a professional speaker, trainer, and author whose experience and insight makes him one of the most sought-after leaders in his field. Utilizing the BRANTA Method™, Rodney helps organizations move from profit-eating compliance programs to profit-saving, logic-based solutions.

One Fortune 500 company requires each of their managers to hear Rodney's message within six-months of their promotion. By combining real life examples and humor, he drives home a message everyone can understand. His interactive presentations expose the myths of traditional management while delivering simple, effective tools. Companies who have implemented the BRANTA Method have reported:

- *a safer workplace*

- *increased morale*

- *more time to concentrate on business, and*

- *greater control over the future.*

DEFEND YOUR PROFITS...
And create an environment that balances productivity, quality and safety.

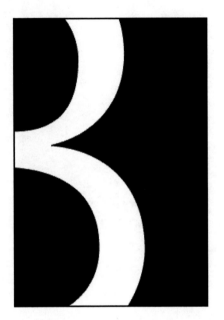

LEARN

What People Are Saying About Rodney!

"Rodney puts the emphasis right where it belongs: on the supervisor."

Mike Wolter
Corporate Director of Safety
Skyline Industries

"Rodney's presentation was informative and hilarious. The audience was engaged from start to finish."

Jayme Finley
HR Administrator
Cal Poly SLO

"We learned more in 30 minutes today with Rodney then we did in the last 9 years with our loss control provider."

Russ Williamson
Division Manager
Skyline Homes

"Rodney inspired our Managers, Supervisors and Committee Members; motivating them to take the next step in the safety process at Constellation Wines US."

Morgan LeBlanc
Corporate Safety Manager
Constellation Wines US

"Mr. Grieve's keynote address set an inspirational tone for the day."

Jerry Bach
Vice President
The Safety Center

LEAD

What People Are Saying About The BRANTA Method!

"Our OSHA rate has dropped by over 50% since Rodney started training our managers in April of 2001. Each month, he delivers his very practical 3 E's of Safety in a manner that is engaging, entertaining and educational. He combines platform skills, regulatory knowledge, and real life experience to inspire our managers to view workplace safety in a new light."

Steven Hood
Manager, Corporate Safety Training
Applied Materials

"I love it! This book is packed with real life tools for any human resources manager responsible for occupational safety."

Karen O'Hara
Owner
HRtoGo

"This is the one minute manager and safety handbook all wrapped into one."

Mark Zachary
Corporate Safety Manager
CH2M Hill OMI

"This is excellent training for supervisors, much more then "just safety". Rodney will take your program SOAR'ing to new heights!"

Charles Boettger
Risk Control Advisor
CCCMRMIA

SOAR

BRANTA Worldwide
Services

It is not about safety! Safety struggles are just symptoms of leadership gaps. Like any skill, leadership is a learned behavior. Believe it or not, every organization has a leadership development process in place. That process might be a formal program that promotes positive reinforcement and solid leadership skills, or may be an informal process that unintentionally reinforces yesterday's management styles and motivational techniques.

One way to close the leadership gap is to provide your management team with the skills and tools necessary to redefine success. BRANTA Worldwide provides powerful and effective tools that put your company on the road to increased safety, quality and productivity:

- *On-Site Leadership Development Programs*
- *Company Meeting Facilitation*
- *Facilitator Certification in the BRANTA Method*
- *Conference Keynote and Break-out Group Presentations*

For more information about these services, or to order additional books or CD's of BRANTA Worldwide presentations, contact us at 866.427.2682 or visit our website: www.branta.com.

BRANTA Worldwide
We help your company safely produce a quality product.